W9-CBF-918

from Collection

11/13/14

Louisburg Library District No. 1

206 S. Broadway

Louisburg, KS. 66053

913-837-2217

www.louisburglibrary.org

CLIMATE CRISIS

Ecosystems at Risk

Stephen Aitken

Cavendish
Square
New York

Louisburg Library
Bringing People and Information Together

Special thanks to Jamison Ervin, a conservation specialist and a project manager with the United Nations Development Programme, for her expert review of this manuscript.

Published in 2014 by Cavendish Square Publishing, LLC
303 Park Avenue South, Suite 1247, New York, NY 10010

Copyright © 2014 by Cavendish Square Publishing, LLC

First Edition

No part of this publication may be reproduced, stored in a retrieval system, or transmitted in any form or by any means—electronic, mechanical, photocopying, recording, or otherwise—without the prior permission of the copyright owner. Request for permission should be addressed to Permissions, Cavendish Square Publishing, 303 Park Avenue South, Suite 1247, New York, NY 10010. Tel (877) 980-4450; fax (877) 980-4454.

Website: cavendishsq.com

This publication represents the opinions and views of the author based on his or her personal experience, knowledge, and research. The information in this book serves as a general guide only. The author and publisher have used their best efforts in preparing this book and disclaim liability rising directly or indirectly from the use and application of this book.

CPSIA Compliance Information: Batch #WS13CSQ

All websites were available and accurate when this book was sent to press.

Library of Congress Cataloging-in-Publication Data

Aitken, Stephen, 1953-
Ecosystems at risk / Stephen Aitken.
    p. cm. — (Climate crisis)
Includes bibliographical references and index.
Summary: "Provides comprehensive information on climate change and its effects on the world's ecosystems"—Provided by publisher.
ISBN 978-1-60870-463-7 (hardcover)
ISBN 978-1-62712-043-2 (paperback)
ISBN 978-1-60870-634-1 (ebook)
1. Climate changes—Juvenile literature. 2. Climate changes—Environmental aspects—Juvenile literature. I. Title. II. Series.
QC903.15.A583 2013
551.6—dc23
2011025243

Editor: Christine Florie
Art Director: Anahid Hamparian
Series Designer: Nancy Sabato

Photo research by Laurie Platt Winfrey, Carousel Research, Inc.

The photographs in this book are used by permission and through the courtesy of:
Alamy: Franz Lanting Studio, 4; Arco Images GmbH, 6, 33; M. Scott Brauer, 37. *Ardea:* Suzie Eszterhas, 23. *Cutcaster:* Sidebar background details. *Getty Images:* Joel Sartore/National Geographic, 51; AFP, 52. *Minden Pictures:* Mitsuaki Iwago, 20; Tui de Roy, 21; Neil Lucas, 25. *Newscom:* Gregory Tervel/AFP,13; Deshakalyan Chowdhur/AFP, 30. *Reuters:* Denis Sarrazin/Center for Northern Studies, 11. *Superstock:* Minden Pictures, Titlepage, 15, 40-41, 43, 46-47; Peter Barritt, 8-9; NHPA, 16-17; Ben Mangor, 26-27; Picture Colour Library, 34-35; All Canada Photos, 38.

Printed in the United States of America

Contents

Library District No. 1
Louisburg Library
206 S. Broadway
Louisburg, KS 66053

Introduction

No single item can define an ecosystem, neither can the sum of its individual parts. An **ecosystem** is the product of a complex series of interactions between living and nonliving things. It is the intricate nature of these relationships that makes it so difficult to predict how individual ecosystems will react to climate change. However, there is little doubt that changes are taking place in ecosystems from the polar regions to the tropics and everywhere in between.

Biodiversity refers to the variety of species within a given environment. Healthy ecosystems with a high level of naturally occurring biodiversity can absorb the impact of climate change more readily than those with fewer species, particularly when key members of the latter are endangered. For example, the extinction of a key species in a simple ecosystem with a small **food web** can be a huge blow to the stability of the system. In an intact, richly biodiverse environment, the extinction of the same species might result in the quick adaptation of a similar species to fill the void and stabilize the ecosystem.

All over the world, ecosystems are at risk due to climate change. Emperor penguins gather near a crack in the sea ice in Antarctica.

A change in the temperature or in the components of the earth's atmospheric layer, such as might take place during a period of rapid climate change, affects all species in all ecosystems. Ecosystems in mountainous regions, at the poles, and on small islands are particularly vulnerable to environmental change. In these regions where climate change is likely to have a major impact, species unable to adapt are at risk of extinction. Because the polar regions play a key role in the control and management of global climate patterns, environmental change at the poles can dramatically affect all other ecosystems.

Ecosystems that contain many species often have high numbers of **endemic** species, irreplaceable species not found anywhere else in the world. When climate change occurs in these rich, biodiverse ecosystems, high species loss can result. For this reason, many **conservationists** are determined to protect the world's biodiversity "hot spots," regions of the world that contain a large number of these unique species. When the population of a species becomes very low, it is designated "endangered" because the genetic variety becomes so small that it is very difficult for the population to recover. Larger population sizes offer more variety for interbreeding and thus result in higher survival rates for the species.

Isolated ecosystems, such as those on oceanic islands, are also home to many endemic species. The Galápagos Islands, off the coast of Ecuador in South America, the location of Charles Darwin's first studies in evolution, have earned protected status because of the large number of unique species living there. However, extreme weather events, changing patterns of precipitation, rising temperatures, ocean acidification (the changing chemistry of ocean waters due to the large amount of carbon dioxide absorbed from

The marine iguana, the only sea-going lizard, is found exclusively on the Galápagos Islands off the coast of Ecuador in South America.

the atmosphere), and rising sea levels—all contribute to the high risk that island ecosystems and their plants and animals endure in a warming world.

Climate change has the ability to affect all ecosystems, no matter how remote or isolated. As the health and stability of an ecosystem is negatively affected, whether it is located in the Arctic, in the Antarctic, on an island or mountain slope, the impacts are felt globally. Factors that affect entire regions, such as the warming and acidification of the ocean waters or the melting of the polar **ice caps**, have a great impact on the global environment. Is it any wonder that climate change is considered one of the greatest threats to the earth's biodiversity?

The melting of the surface ice on the Arctic waters exposes the dark ocean. This results in more heat being absorbed from the sun's rays.

Chapter One

Is the Arctic Set to Defrost?

The Arctic region consists of the entire area north of the Arctic Circle, including the North Pole. It plays a vital role in the regulation of the global climate system. The glistening Arctic ice and snow reflect the heat of the sun's rays away from the earth and thus help to keep the rest of the planet cool.

Changes in the North

The impact of climate change in the Arctic environment serves as an early warning system for the rest of the planet. The approximately 4 million Arctic inhabitants are well aware of how quickly their land is changing: spring thaws are arriving earlier, fall freeze-ups are occurring later, extreme weather is more frequent, and the sea ice is rapidly melting. As the melting ice exposes the dark ocean waters, a feedback mechanism is created. The Arctic sea absorbs even more heat from the sun, the result being an increase in the rate of warming of the entire Arctic region.

Researchers report that the Arctic sea ice is melting at an astonishing rate. NASA satellite images show the polar ice cap and the permanent ice cover shrinking at a rate of 9 percent per decade. The three-thousand-year-old Ward Hunt Ice Shelf, the largest single block of ice in the Arctic, started cracking near the end of the twentieth century, and it is now breaking into multiple pieces. The earth's layer of ice and snow, collectively known as the **cryosphere**, is melting.

Long-term studies show that the Arctic sea ice is decreasing in thickness. Multiyear ice (ice that survives summer melts and gets thicker every year) made up about 30 percent of winter sea ice cover in the last two decades of the last century. In September 2012 a new record low was reached for annual summertime minimum extent according to the National Snow and Ice Date Center (NSIDC), almost 300,000 square miles less than the previous low in 2007. Many scientists now believe there is a high probability that the Arctic Ocean will be free of summer ice within two or three decades. NASA reports that the retreat of Arctic sea ice is taking place much faster than predicted and the thickness of the ice is also declining.

The Arctic, which still has some of the earth's largest intact, continuous ecosystems, stores huge amounts of freshwater in its glaciers. Scientists need to understand the Arctic more thoroughly to plot the mechanics of how it influences global climate. The increase in open seawater free from ice is expected to result in significant changes to the Arctic ecosystem. Feedback mechanisms in the Arctic Ocean could lead to a dramatically warmer world, which in turn would melt more land-based ice mass and lead to much higher sea levels.

The Canadian seal-hunting industry has received heavy criticism over the years for the brutal killing of baby seals. However, in the spring of 2010, it was ice conditions, not hunting, that proved fatal to many seal pups. The worst conditions ever recorded in Canada's Gulf of Saint Lawrence—wide-open waters instead of the usual ice floes—resulted in the death of thousands of seal pups. The starving young seals strewn along the beaches of Prince Edward Island provided further proof that the defrosting Arctic is

On July 22, 2008, the Ward Hunt Ice Shelf began a wave of disintegration. By August a total of 83 square miles (214 sq km) had been lost.

affecting regions well beyond its immediate vicinity. Lack of ice is leaving mother seals with few locations to bear their young or feed their pups.

Arctic Animals

Today the Arctic fox is classified as an endangered species in Norway, where only one hundred individuals remain. The dark-eyed, white-haired fox is being used as an **indicator species** to study the impacts of climate change on the Arctic ecosystem. At the end of the last century, the Arctic fox population in the Norwegian mountains and northern coastal areas was in the thousands; today there is the possibility that the species may disappear altogether.

Methane, a powerful greenhouse gas, has reached its highest concentration in the Arctic in the past 400,000 years.

Other species at the top of the food chain in the Norwegian tundra are the snowy owl, the rough-legged buzzard, and three species of Arctic skua. The loss of a single species can be disastrous for such delicate ecosystems. In Norway, a narrow strip of land separates the northern forest and the Arctic sea areas. As the climate warms, the forest is moving north and may eventually consume the entire Norwegian Arctic tundra ecosystem.

Many animal and bird species migrate to the Arctic from other parts of the world. The migrational patterns of some Arctic seabirds that usually winter in California and Mexico are changing because of the warm Arctic surface air temperatures. The brant, a small Pacific sea goose, typically winters in Mexico, but a U.S. Geological Survey (USGS) study found that up to 30 percent of brant populations now forgo the migration altogether and just stay in Alaska. The reason? Warmer temperatures in Alaska have re-

The arctic fox is critically engandered in Norway, Sweden, and Finland due to loss of prey.

duced the coastal sea ice to such an extent that the brant's favorite food, eelgrass, has become increasingly accessible.

In 1997 fewer than 3,000 brant geese persevered through an Alaskan winter, and now records show as many as 40,000 remain. Researchers expect the Pacific brant numbers to increase in Alaska as long as temperatures keep warming and the coastal sea ice continues to melt. Scientists warn that if there is a sudden extended period of cold weather that locks up the sea ice, the entire population of Pacific brant could be in danger.

The poster animal for the ravages of climate change in the Arctic environment is the polar bear. Few images are as dramatic as this huge, powerful animal helplessly peering out at the disappearing ice. The polar bear after all is designed for success on sea ice, right down to the color camouflage. Almost all of this great mammal's needs and activities are dependent on sea ice, including seal hunting, transportation, refuge, finding mates, and breeding. The loss of ice is so critical to the survival of po-

CASE STUDY

CARIBOU IN GLOBAL DECLINE

Caribou herds roam the cold lands of Alaska, Canada, and Greenland. They have adapted to the cold climate of the Arctic, where they are the most common grazing animal. Caribou are undergoing a climate change crisis. Recent data indicate that of fifty-eight herds in the northern hemisphere, thirty-four are declining in number, and only eight are increasing (no data exists on the sixteen remaining herds). The trend downward is surprisingly consistent across the whole northern hemisphere, at a rate and pattern in sync with Arctic temperature increases and man-made landscape changes.

Researchers believe that increased insect activity, reduction in winter fat storage, and other environmental impacts are negatively affecting caribou herds. In recent years, the imposition of hunting restrictions have helped ease the pressure on caribou populations.

Polar bears depend on sea ice for their survival. Melting ice jeopardizes their future.

lar bear populations that the U.S. Fish and Wildlife Service (FWS) listed polar bears as a threatened species in 2008. Despite the fact that close to 75 percent of the world's polar bears reside in Canada, to date, only the province of Manitoba has declared the animal a threatened species. Most polar bear managers and **climatologists** agree that if current trends continue, the polar bear will be gone from much of its range by 2050, with only one-third of the population remaining—a mere seven thousand to eight thousand individuals.

Of the 19 circumpolar populations of polar bears, 8 groups are declining in number.

Many of the polar bears may move farther north, where conditions could be more favorable to their lifestyle. In the meantime, before climate change can be brought under control, conservationists suggest that other threats to this animal can be minimized by protecting the areas where they build their dens and by reducing hunting and other human disturbances.

Research shows that the Antarctic has the fastest warming trends in the Southern Hemisphere.

Chapter Two

Antarctica—Afloat in the Southern Ocean

If the Arctic is a frozen ocean surrounded by land, then the Antarctic is a frozen land surrounded by ocean. The Southern Ocean (also called the Antarctic Ocean) is a vast body of water that isolates the continent of Antarctica from its neighbors. The Antarctic Convergence, a highly effective biological barrier, is formed at the point where the cold Antarctic waters meet with warmer waters from the north. This barrier serves to make the Southern Ocean a substantially closed ecosystem, one that maintains itself without external input. The vast Southern Ocean also ensures that no land predators, such as the Arctic polar bear, exist in Antarctica.

Studying Change in Antarctica

Antarctica is the earth's coldest, windiest, and driest continent. Much less is known about the Antarctic than its northern cousin, the Arctic, and even less understood is how it has such a profound effect on the global climate. Fortunately, because of limited direct human influence, the Antarctic has been relatively unspoiled when compared with most places on earth. Climate change, however, is affecting even this remotest of regions.

The Antarctic Peninsula is actually a mountain range, considered an extension of the Andes system in South America. Averaging more than 6,500 feet (2,000 m) high, with snow-free areas during the summer season, this region is the Antarctic's warmest part. It contains habitats that support microbes, insects, breeding grounds for some marine mammals and birds, and the only two flowering plants on the continent. The Antarctic continent is warming at a rate faster than any region in the entire Southern Hemisphere.

The Southern Ocean absorbs significant amounts of both heat and carbon dioxide (CO_2). Air temperatures in the Antarctic Peninsula have increased 5 degrees Fahrenheit, or 2.8 degrees Celsius, since record-keeping began fifty years ago. Climatologists worry that if temperatures continue to rise, the melting of Antarctic **ice sheets** could create a significant rise in global sea levels. Also, there are signs that marine life, adapted to the frigid Antarctic waters, is affected by rising Antarctic temperatures. Studies show that seals, albatross, and penguins produce fewer young in a warmer ocean.

With an average precipitation of only two inches per year, the Antarctic continent is covered by a 7 million cubic mile (29 million km³) ice sheet. A rise in atmospheric temperatures is causing a slow but steady slide of ice sheets into the sea. Reports show that most of Antarctica's glaciers along the west coast are decreasing in size, and during the last twelve years the glacial retreat has accelerated. Only a few glaciers are increasing in size, and that increase is due to increased regional precipitation.

The polar regions lock ice away, keep sea levels low, and serve to cool the effects of rising air temperatures on the rest of the planet. The Antarctic and the Arctic regions exchange subtle climate signals, transmitted by the currents that develop in the Southern Ocean and circulate to the rest of the world. Warm Southern Ocean surface waters sink as they increase in density owing to the **brine** rejected from sea ice formation. This creates deep ocean currents that appear like a giant ocean conveyor belt. As the conveyor connects the warm surface and cold deep-ocean waters, heat and salt are transported around the world's oceans, and nearby land is warmed at the same time.

The Antarctic in a Warming World

Many scientists are predicting that by 2100 the West Antarctic ice sheet, a land-based ice mass, could discharge enough ice to raise sea levels as much as 4.5 feet (1.4 m). This would be disastrous for communities located in coastal regions around the world. According to a December 2012 paper in *Nature Geoscience*, Central West Antarctica has one of the fastest warming rates on earth, three times the global average. Owing to the important role they play in cooling the earth, these effects could have major consequences for the rest of the world.

Though the main Antarctic continent has one of the most extreme climates in the world, the western side of the peninsula is warmer and moist, as are the sub-Antarctic islands. The **flora** in these areas is much more

A retreating glacier in the Ross Sea area in Antarctica.

diverse, and a few terrestrial vertebrates even live on the islands. Predictions for a warmer future could see these ecosystems expand their diversity to include new species migrating from the north.

Antarctic Animals

Penguins are the most common bird in Antarctica. Awkward on land, they are at home in the water where they spend three-quarters of their time. Studies show that over the past fifty years emperor penguins, the largest living penguin species, have declined in number by 50 percent. Researchers believe that the decline is due to a loss of sea ice in the late 1970s caused by a sustained warm period. Less

TIME TO ACT fact!

Emperor penguins breed on the sea ice, which needs to be thick enough to persist until the chicks are grown. Adélie and emperor penguins are relocating farther and farther south.

Emperor penguins, both mature adults and developing young, gather to form a colony on the frozen sea ice of Antarctica.

ice means fewer krill, a main staple in the diet of emperor penguins and other ocean dwellers.

Penguins maintain body heat through several layers of feathers as well as a layer of body fat under the skin. They are so efficient at staying warm that overheating becomes a problem in the summer months. How they will do in the warmer Antarctic climate of the future is a major concern to conservationists.

Warmer temperatures negatively affect elephant seals and some albatross species. As with many other species dealing with climate change in other parts of the world, historical records show that the Adélie penguins adapt by changing their migration patterns. The question is, will they be able to adapt quickly enough?

Birds—of the Flying Sort

The albatross is in danger of extinction. Living up to sixty years of age, this great wanderer has the remarkable ability to filter out salt from seawa-

ECOSYSTEMS ON THE ANTARCTIC CONTINENT

Few species can survive the harsh conditions of the rugged Antarctic continent, but those that do form some of the simplest ecosystems ever known.

The only continental **fauna** are simple insects. In terms of fauna, these are the least diverse habitats on the earth. There are seventeen species of penguins in total, but only two, the emperor and Adélie penguins, make their true home on the Antarctic continent.

With permanent ice and snow covering 99 percent of the continent, less than one percent of the land area is available for plants to reproduce.

Black-browed albatross parents stand guard over their nesting chicks.

ter through a special gland in its beak. This specialized gland allows the albatross to survive long journeys across ocean waters. The albatross is particularly vulnerable since it has one of the lowest reproductive rates of any bird. Some species, such as the black-browed albatross, feed on a diet consisting mainly of krill. With warming waters putting further pressure on the food sources, the impact of climate change on already declining populations will be increased.

Despite the shortage of nesting grounds, other seabirds play an important role in the marine ecosystem of Antarctica. The snow petrel is one of the most plentiful species, but fulmars, skuas, and shearwaters also dominate. All Antarctic birds are vulnerable to environmental change, in that their low reproductive rates make it difficult for them to recover from population declines.

Marine Mammals

Whales and seals play a vital role in the marine ecosystem of the Southern Ocean. The sperm whale is the largest of the toothed whales, a group that includes killer and fourtooth whales and bottlenose and other dolphins. Baleen whales include the gigantic blue whale (the largest animal on earth), the humpback whale, the fin whale, the sei whale, the southern right whale, and the minke whale, a species that spends much of its time right underneath the ice, feeding on krill.

The whales arrive for a period of rich feeding, but when the Antarctic waters become too cold and set with ice, most of these whales head to warmer waters to calve their young. Scientists are still studying how warming surface waters of the Southern Ocean affect the migratory patterns of the giant whales, but one thing is clear—it will have a significant impact on the ecosystem balance.

Seals also have two natural groups: true seals and eared seals (fur seals and sea lions). All seals have ears; on true seals the ear is just a small opening on the side of the head, while on eared seals, there are small external structures. The four species that may be affected by sea-ice loss are the leopard, Ross, Weddell, and crabeater seals, all of which are dependent on ice habitats.

As the climate changes and sea ice declines, Weddell seals will be greatly affected.

The rapid rate at which climate change is taking place does not allow enough time for species to adapt, either by evolutionary change, which can take up to hundreds of thousands of years, or by changing their location. Antarctica is like a dangling icicle, delicately balanced at the southern pole of the earth. A few more degrees of warming could send this ecosystem into a downward spiral that would have a major impact on global climate patterns.

The world's islands and their surrounding waters often contain rich reservoirs of unique plants and animals.

Chapter Three

Islands—
Disappearing Worlds

There are more than 100,000 islands scattered throughout the world's ocean waters; these islands are much more than just a place for a pleasant vacation under swaying palm trees. Islands are a source of high biological diversity and are often home to plants and animals not found anywhere else in the world. The ocean waters surrounding islands harbor half of the marine species on the planet.

The conservation status of island flora and fauna is indicative of the poor record of protection island life has received. The endangerment level of these species is particularly high compared with that in other regions of the world. Records of recent animal extinctions show that 75 percent occurred on islands—a very high number. In the United States alone, three-quarters of all plant and animal extinctions have taken place in Hawaii.

Marine biologists estimate that 70 percent of all coral reefs will be gone in fifty years, owing largely to coral bleaching (from high surface-water temperatures) and ocean acidification—both a direct result of high CO_2 emissions. Mangrove forests, natural buffers between the land and the sea, are rapidly becoming the victims of coastal development, fish and shrimp farms, and rising sea levels. With the disappearance of half of the world's mangrove forests, many islands have been exposed to the ravages of the sea.

Island Life Amid Rising Waters

The specific effects of climate change and the severity of the impact will vary from island to island, but sea level rise is probably the single biggest threat. The seas are rising higher owing largely to **thermal expansion**, resulting in an increase in ocean volume. The melting of polar ice caps and ice shelves, and receding mountain glaciers are all contributing to rising sea levels. Many islands are only 10 to 13 feet (3–4 m) above sea level, and most of the buildings, roads, and economic activity are located near the coast. Rising seas cause eroded coastlines, loss of habitable land, and infiltration of seawater into freshwater sources.

The islands most immediately at risk from rising sea levels are the Maldives, in the Indian Ocean; Kiribati and the Marshall Islands, in the central Pacific Ocean; and Tuvalu and Tokelau, in the South Pacific. Though some islands have regions with higher elevations and may not be in danger of total submersion in the near future, their low-lying coastal areas may be lost permanently to the sea. Inland areas may be swamped and fertile land submerged. Loss of shorelines are expected on virtually all islands. Coastal areas of all continents will also be affected, including millions of people in heavily populated cities, including Venice, Los Angeles, and Amsterdam, and many others located close to sea level.

The Carteret Islands of Papua New Guinea have been losing land to the sea steadily in recent years. The government has a voluntary evacuation plan in place, but some scientists predict these islands will be completely uninhabitable by 2015. The social effects on these islands may be a preview of what is to come on a larger scale as climate change grows in impact around the world. The Carteret Islands may go down in history as the former home of the first climate change refugees.

Islands are also highly vulnerable to natural disasters such as intense tropical storms, flooding, tsunamis, and cyclones. The poor condition of some islands' coral reefs leaves them more vulnerable to extreme weather events, particularly storms and tsunamis. The Indian Ocean tsunami of 2004 was a rude awakening to this fact; it completely devastated coastal communities of small islands in the Indian Ocean, including the Maldives and the Andaman and Nicobar Islands. In just a few hours over 283,000 people were dead, and more than a million people were displaced from their homes and communities. Coastal areas where mangrove forests and coral reefs were degraded or absent altogether were the most affected. The Intergovern-

Extensive damage to the natural vegetation on Great Nicobar Island took place after a tsunami struck in 2004.

mental Panel on Climate Change (IPCC) predicts that there will be an increase in the intensity and frequency of extreme weather events, which will cause widespread damage to island infrastructure and agriculture.

Islands often have many plants and animals that are found nowhere else in the world because of millions of years of evolution in isolation from mainland species and often in unique environmental and climatic conditions. However, owing to their small size and often simple food chains, the biodiversity of islands can be extremely fragile. Rising temperatures are likely to upset this delicate balance.

A reduction in the availability of fresh water because of **salinization** of soils and water sources from seawater infiltration is likely to be one of the most devastating impacts of sea level rises on island nations. This can lead to reduced agricultural capacity and loss of food security.

TIME TO ACT fact!

In October 2009 the Maldivian president and his ministers held an underwater cabinet meeting as a symbolic call to the world to assist all island nations by lowering CO_2 emissions.

The impact of climate change on Madagascar's lemur population (see page 32) may very well be an indication of things to come for other tropical ecosystems and their endemic species. At the end of this century, the earth may have far fewer living species than it had when the century started.

Island Nations—Looking for Change

Island leaders are aware that if greenhouse gas emissions are significantly reduced today, it will still be fifty years before climate change runs its course. The islanders believe that industrial nations are the root cause of global warming; however, they refuse to take definitive steps to prevent it. Small island nations emit less than one percent of global greenhouse gases, yet the land on which they live could be lost forever as a result of rising sea levels.

> **TIME TO ACT fact!**
>
> The surrounding coral reef of the U.S. Virgin Islands is showing signs of bleaching. Increasingly intense storms, along with rising sea levels, are eroding beaches and coastlines.

Island life depends upon the importation of many basic necessities, such as food and fuel. Added costs of transportation often make these basics enormously expensive, particularly with rising and unpredictable gas prices. These financial pressures have stimulated what might be one of the few good outcomes of climate change on island life—plans to reduce island dependence on petroleum. With the additional pressure of increasing populations, many island states are getting serious about developing renewable resources such as wind turbines, solar panels, and hydroelectric and geothermal power.

CASE STUDY

MADAGASCAR—CLIMATE CHANGE IN THE LAND OF LEMURS

Madagascar, an island off the southeastern coast of Africa, is in the midst of a silent climate crisis. Along with several surrounding islands, its isolation from mainland Africa has resulted in a great number of endemic plant and animal species. About 70 percent of the estimated 250,000 species, including most of its mammals, half of its birds, and the majority of its plants, are unique to the island, the fourth largest island on earth (after Greenland, New Guinea, and Borneo).

Madagascar is the only place on earth where lemurs live in the wild. However, climate change could deliver a fatal blow to the island's endangered lemur populations. Dr. Patricia Wright, a **primatologist** at the State University of New York, has closely studied the impact of climate change on endangered lemurs in Madagascar's Ranomafana National Park. Rising temperatures and dry conditions are having a particularly adverse affect on the Milne-Edwards' sifakas (lemurs). Because of the dry, hot conditions, the mother lemurs are not producing as much milk as they used to, and the infant survival rate has dropped.

The greater bamboo lemur (below), has been reduced to about one hundred individuals as a result of hunting and habitat loss. The final blow to the species could well be climate change, which is causing a reduction in rainfall, the drying of rivers, and fewer watershed bamboo plants.

Research indicates that as earth warms, mountain life will move high in altitude to try to reach cooler habitats.

Mountain Ecosystems— Islands in the Sky

Mountain areas cover close to one-quarter of the earth's land surface. It is a well-established fact that as temperatures rise, many plants and animals move to higher, cooler habitats on mountainsides. A few thousand feet in elevation can mean substantial reductions in temperature. Mountain areas are, in effect, islands, disconnected from each other by wide expanses of land that are often developed for agriculture and other uses. Species cannot easily travel to other "islands in the sky" when their habitat becomes unsuitable.

Chapter Four

Glaciers

Mountains provide water for more than half the world's population; glaciers contain almost 70 percent of the freshwater on earth. The meltwater from the snow and ice in glaciers flows into rivers and streams all over the world. With rising global temperatures, the amount and timing of the runoff is changing. In many cases it is coming earlier in the spring, and as a result, streams and rivers are dry by the late summer months, when the water is desperately needed. Less snow on the hills means a smaller supply of life-giving water, water that is going to be in even greater demand as world populations continue to grow. In addition, melting glaciers expose dark rock, which absorbs more heat from the sun than snow and ice. This feedback loop is increasing the rate of melting of the world's glaciers.

The Himalayan glaciers, which contain the largest concentration of nonpolar ice in the world, supply water to all of the major rivers in Asia. All over the world glaciers are melting, and photographers and glaciologists are recording the startling changes in depth of snow and the icy-tongued reaches of the glaciers themselves. The largest glaciers in Glacier National Park, in Montana, have been reduced to just one-third of the size they were in 1850. Some researchers predict they could disappear completely in the next thirty years.

Mountain Ecosystems

Changes in the water cycle are not the only effect of higher temperatures on mountain ecosystems. The tree line, the elevation to which trees will grow

> ### TIME TO ACT fact!
>
> Glaciers in the European Alps have shrunk to half their size over the last century. In Africa only 8 percent of Mount Kenya's largest glacier remains.

Hikers stand at the base of Grinnell Glacier in Montana's Glacier National Park.

on mountainsides, is rising. Trees are rapidly invading many high-altitude meadows that were once awash in multicolored alpine wildflowers. Plants and animals in many mountain ecosystems are moving to higher elevations to find cooler habitats.

Few things in the science of climatology are as certain as the extinction of many of the world's mountain-dwelling species. Climatologists are certain about this dire prediction for three reasons: first, the effect of temperature increases on mountain ecosystems can be readily calculated, and historical data exists; second, the tolerance to change of many mountain-dwelling species is well known; third, the heights of mountain peaks have been measured—and hence, given the rate of warming, the time to extinction can be calculated. Animals under threat as their mountain habitats disappear to climate change include the Australian mountain pygmy possum, the ptarmigan, the snow bunting, the marmot, the American pika, the Gelada baboon (in Ethiopia), and the monarch butterfly (in Mexico).

Many scientists predict that the earth will get at least 3 degrees hotter this century, and if current CO_2 emission levels continue, temperatures may rise as high as 7 degrees relative to 1980–1990 temperatures. In New Guinea, the highest peak is just over 16,000 feet. A rise of 7 degrees may very well push the last of New Guinea's alpine habitats off the summit. With such extreme changes in temperature possible (the Intergovernmental Panel on Climate Change upper limit prediction is 11.5 degrees), there are few mountains anywhere on earth high enough to provide refuge for these alpine species. A rise of only a few degrees in earth's average temperature could result in the loss of many mountain species.

Warmer temperatures are also increasing the frequency and intensity of forest fires in mountain areas. Megafires are on the rise; 2011 saw the worst fires in the history of Arizona, with the Wallow Fire destroying more than 538,000 acres of forest. Every year brings more evidence of this effect. According to the BC Wildfire Management Branch a total of 1,605 wildfires burned in the year 2012, at a total cost of $155 million.

The snow bunting is under threat as temperatures rise in its mountain home.

Many climatologists predict that the impact of climate change on mountain ecosystems is a preview of what to expect in lowland environments. Information on the health of mountain ecosystems and the ability to track the impact of changes can therefore assist in the development of management strategies for other areas. Mountain birds are excellent indicators of change. They follow the shifts in vegetation as plants slowly move up mountainsides to meet their temperature and precipitation requirements. Studies show that extinction risk is greatest for bird species with narrow ranges in altitude; that is, those that can survive only at very specific elevations. Globally, hundreds of mountain bird species are in peril because of rising temperatures; some species can move to neighboring mountains, but those in isolated mountain conditions cannot. Sedentary birds, those that do not migrate, are at much greater risk in a warming world than those that migrate. Tropical mountain birds are expected to be particularly hard hit. Researchers estimate that for each 1 degree increase in global average temperature, one hundred bird species will go extinct.

The vulnerability of species to climate change in mountainous environments can be seen clearly through simple geometry. The circumference of a mountain is largest at its base and smallest at its summit. Higher elevation areas are therefore smaller in terms of actual land area. As plants and animals move higher to find cooler habitats, they are competing with native species for an ever decreasing amount of land. Competition continues to increase between species for light, air, nutrients, and food sources as temperatures rise and plants and animals continue to seek what can be their only refuge, a shrinking island in the sky.

A Henkel's leaf-tailed gecko rests on a tree in Madagascar, one of the world's biodiversity hot spots.

Chapter Five

Biodiversity Hot Spots

The variety of life on earth is not spread evenly over the surface of the planet. Certain regions, particularly in the warm, moist tropics, contain an enormous number and variety of species. These areas, known as biodiversity hot spots because of the variety and density of their plant and animal life, run the risk of high species loss as a result of climate change.

CASE STUDY

COSTA RICAN CLOUD FORESTS

Costa Rica is famous for its biodiversity and for the active conservation of its rain forests. Protecting Costa Rican ecosystems from the ravages of climate change could prove to be the country's greatest challenge yet. Studies show that many regions of Costa Rica will become drier and warmer, particularly at higher elevations. A mountain range reaching heights close to 10,000 feet runs down the center of the country, flanked by two coastal regions, the Pacific to the west and the Caribbean to the east. The area contains a variety of ecosystems with different temperatures and levels of precipitation, each with unique wildlife. Layers of clouds help the forests retain moisture and allow the plants and animals to survive the high summer temperatures. The height at which these clouds develop is critical to the survival of these ecosystems, particularly as global temperatures rise. If as expected, the cloud layers reposition to higher elevations, lower ecosystems will be left exposed to a warmer, drier climate. Many species are expected to become extinct. Some will survive by moving uphill to reach cooler and wetter habitats. Amphibians, with their sensitive, water-absorbing skin, are one of the most vulnerable groups of animals because of their constant need for moisture.

A study in the Costa Rican protected area La Selva showed that over a period of thirty-five years, both amphibian and reptile populations had declined by 75 percent. The researchers attribute these huge population losses to a dry forest floor as a result of less precipitation. Not only are the drier forests more prone to fire, but the leaf litter that provides much-needed moisture for native frogs, toads, salamanders, and snakes is disappearing.

These apparently small changes in ecosystem structure and function can have wide-reaching effects on which groups of animals and plants are able to survive. Rain forests lack resilience to drying and therefore are particularly vulnerable to climate change. Warmer, drier tropical forests result in more forest fires, which further increase drying, thus creating a feedback loop that augments future warming and increases the impact on tropical ecosystems.

Globally, more than one-third of amphibian species are threatened; since 1980 it is estimated that 120 species have become extinct. Climate change could be the final knockout blow from which amphibians will never recover.

Since many of the species present are unique and highly adapted to their tropical ecosystems, the protection of these areas is a particularly high priority. Madagascar and other Indian Ocean islands are hot spots, as are the tropical Andes.

Conservation International is an environmental organization that has championed the formal designation of biodiversity hot spots. To qualify, a region must contain 1,500 species of endemic **vascular plants**, and it must have already lost 70 percent of its original habitat. By 2010, the thirty-four hot spots that had been designated harbored 44 percent of the world's plants and 35 percent of land vertebrates. These areas present one of humanity's most important challenges—to conserve relatively small sections of the planet's surface to save an enormous number of species, many of which have yet to be classified by scientists.

Protecting Hot Spots

Plants and animals in hot spot areas are already under threat from deforestation and exploitation of natural resources. Climate change adds additional pressure on these ecosystems and may ultimately become the cause of enormous species extinctions. From 1980 to 2000, a total area of farmland the size of Alaska (more than half a million square miles) was created throughout the world, more than 80 percent from the cutting of tropical forests.High priority has to be given to effective protection and management of forested areas so that there is connectivity between areas to allow for the free movement of species as they respond to warmer habitats.

The principle of hot spots is simple. With a limited amount of money available for conservation, protecting threatened regions that are biodiverse and species-rich means that more species will be saved per dollar invested. Climate change impacts have added to the need to provide this protection as quickly as possible.

Degraded areas located near hot spot regions need particular attention to ensure that there is some connection between the protected areas. In addition, new parks and reserves need to be added to those areas that are under high threat or where species are highly endangered. The success of these conservation efforts requires cooperation and strategic planning with the local people and indigenous populations. Many of these communities have a historical relationship with the land areas and their living species, and the livelihood of the local people should be taken into consideration when protecting areas. Research shows that inclusion of local people in the decision-making and management of protected areas improves the chances of success.

TIME TO ACT fact!

Some studies predict that species extinctions in tropical hot spots resulting from global climate change could be even greater than those resulting from deforestation.

This panda cub was bred at a captive breeding preserve in China.

Chapter Six

Giving Nature a Helping Hand

Earth is a survivor. It has successfully weathered more than 4 billion years of challenges that have shaped its atmosphere, landscapes, oceans, and species. Throughout earth's history there have been a number of global-warming events, with extremely high CO_2 levels, that dramatically reshaped the **biosphere**. Earth survived these warming events, though with a much reduced diversity of life forms. Many species went extinct. The current warming event is unique both in the extremely high rate of change and in the cause of that change.

According to an estimated 95 percent of researchers, there is little doubt that the increase in global temperatures and related effects are due to the excessive emission by humans of carbon and other greenhouse gases into the atmosphere.

There are several options available to help ecosystems build resilience to the effects of climate change. Recognizing the important role that protected areas play in conserving species on earth, protected areas have increased in number by 58 percent and in their extent by 48 percent according to the UNEP *Protected Planet Report* 2012. The design and management of national parks, reserves, and conservation areas, including the development of corridors and networks, will be key components in the protection of the earth's flora and fauna from the ravages of climate change.

Preventing Species Extinctions

Each species, whether it be a plant, animal, or insect, is affected by climate change in a different way. The first order of action, if we are to prevent extinctions, is to have reliable information on the status of species populations and on the species that are vulnerable or in danger of extinction. The International Union for Conservation of Nature (IUCN) maintains a database for this purpose. The Red List, updated annually, allows conservationists to see which species are in immediate danger, which are recovering from previous losses, and which may be in trouble in the future. The various categories on the Red List include "least concern," "near threatened," "vulnerable," "endangered," "critically endangered," "extinct in the wild," and "extinct."

There are many reasons that species may be forced down this path, including overhunting, disease, pollution, illegal trade, poaching, deforestation, invasive species, habitat degradation, and global climate change. To take a species that has dwindled to the edge of extinction and turn it back into a viable, sustainable population can be an expensive process. There are two main ways to do this: "in situ"—working directly in the ecosystem— and "ex situ," in a controlled situation, or out of the environment.

In situ methods of protection demand a practical look at the primary causes of species endangerment and strive to relieve the pressure on species before the population declines too far. Providing them safe refuge is the most important requirement, but allowing animals to move freely between protected areas is quickly becoming a vital element in planning and designing for climate change.

Ex-situ methods of species protection are used when the threat of extinction is severe. These methods involve programs such as captive breeding, propagation (building a sustainable population), and assisted reintroduction of individuals back into the wild. These processes are not economically feasible for all endangered species, so zoologists sometimes have to make difficult choices of which species to save. Often the position of the species in the food web and its role in the ecosystem become determining factors.

Another management technique that **ecologists** use is assisted colonization (sometimes called managed relocation). The idea is to move a population of seriously threatened animals or plants to new areas (often nearby) that have similar but more suitable habitats. Natural dispersal to these new locations is often restricted by human use of the landscape and by barriers to movement. Many ecologists are hesitant to recommend a relocation program because of the danger of introducing animals into an environment that, in the absence of predators, could take over and crowd out native species.

Can Species Be Saved by Captive Breeding?

A number of zoos have started to assist endangered wild animal populations through species survival plans (SSPs). These programs manage breeding to create self-sustaining populations that are large enough to be genetically diverse and demographically stable; that is, to have a proper balance between younger and older animals. The ultimate objective is to reintroduce the captive-bred animal back into its native habitat and rebuild the population to a level that can continue to thrive on its own. According to the Association of Zoos and Aquariums (AZA), SSPs over the past three decades have successfully revived endangered populations of red wolves and California condors.

In this time of enormous pressure on biodiversity, the AZA is managing more than 115 SSPs with more than 180 species affected, many of them well-known animals such as giant pandas and lowland gorillas.

Protected Areas

One of the primary threats for species in the wild is the degradation or destruction of the environments they live in. National and provincial parks, conservation areas, reserves, marine protected areas, no-hunting zones—all attempt to protect natural habitats and their species to varying degrees. The proper management and maintenance of these areas, as well as the establishment of new protected areas in regions of high priority and endangered biodiversity, will determine how many species are able to survive in a warming world.

Rising global temperatures are changing ecosystems around the world, including those of protected areas. An area established to protect plant and

The Quino Checkerspot

Assisted colonizations need to be considered on an individual basis. Some researchers are seriously considering the relocation of the endangered Quino checkerspot butterfly from the scrubland of southern California to nearby mountain ranges. In this case the scientists feel there is a good certainty that the butterfly would have relocated on its own to escape an inhospitable habitat were it not for human-made barriers to its movement and dispersal. This would be a relatively small project compared with, for instance, moving a population of pika, small mountain-dwelling animals that do not fare well in a warming climate, from one mountain environment to another. Researchers have come up with definite criteria to rank the practicality of an undertaking; considerations include how close to extinction the species is and how much the relocation will cost. In the case of the checkerspot butterfly, a few days' labor to relocate a small insect population is a relatively small-scale experiment, but actions such as these might become much more commonplace in the future. As the planet warms, the need for species to find safer, cooler climates is only going to grow. The survival of many animals and plants may very well depend on whatever helping hand humans can give them.

A baby western lowland gorilla naps on its mother at the Taranga Zoo in Sydney, Australia.

animal species that no longer find that area habitable is not serving its purpose. These protected areas must be reassessed in the light of climate change. Though natural evolution and change are an integral part of our national parks, climate change will fundamentally transform them in the not-too-distant future.

Research shows that Montana's Glacier National Park, one of the oldest parks in the United States, will lose its glaciers within the next four decades. In California, Joshua Tree National Park may need a name change. The Joshua tree, which needs an occasional winter cold snap to flower and seed, is expected to be extinct in the wild by the end of this century because of a rapidly warming western U.S. climate.

By creating networks of safe havens across the landscape, species that are able to respond to climate change by shifting their ranges are able to do so. Degraded habitats need to be restored to a healthy condition to allow corridors of movement between habitable areas. As landscapes become more and more fragmented in a world of rising human populations, connectivity between wild and protected areas is becoming increasingly important and may be the only way to save and build upon the protected area systems already in place.

THE BLACK-FOOTED FERRET

The black mask across the face and the slender black feet characterize this endangered member of the weasel family—the only native ferret in North America. These ferocious little masked rodents can dig out their major prey—prairie dogs—with remarkable speed. One black-footed ferret consumes up to a hundred prairie dogs a year, along with a supplementary diet of small rodents, rabbits, and birds. Living underground in their burrows 90 percent of the time, native ferrets are completely dependent on prairie dog populations for survival. Historically, the black-footed ferret's range extended across the western intermountain and prairie grasslands region all the way from Canada to Mexico. From a population in the tens of thousands, the numbers dwindled to a mere eighteen in 1986, largely owing to habitat destruction. In 1996 the black-footed ferret was categorized as "extinct in the wild." Conservation efforts have been attempting to restore the wild population, and since 1985, more than six thousand black-footed ferrets have been born in captivity.

Prairie dogs, however, are now rapidly declining in number owing to a combination of habitat destruction, extermination by farmers and hunters, and the burden of unusual diseases. Conservationists are worried that the effects of climate change on the black-footed ferret's major prey might prevent the recovery of the wild population. Droughts brought on by climate change are expected to reduce the grassland plants that the prairie dogs need for food, increase the frequency of fires, and augment the threat of invasive species. The decline in prairie dog populations does not bode well for the restoration of the beleaguered black-footed ferret.

What Can You Do?

The most important contribution that any one person can make to prevent additional climate change is to reduce the use of fossil fuels. The most common uses are for heating, air conditioning, electricity, and fuel for vehicles.

One of the first steps a person can take is to switch to green energy. Install a programmable thermostat so that heat and air conditioning are not wasted when they are not required. Dress warmly at home so the thermostat can be reduced a few degrees, turn lights off when not in use, replace bulbs and showerheads with energy-efficient ones, and walk or use bicycles for short errands instead of using the car.

Most people do not know that there are many hidden petroleum products in their lives. These products, which include shampoo, deodorant, makeup, and cleaning products, can be exchanged for ones that are more environmentally friendly. Avoid products containing acetone, benzene, methylene chloride, parabens, petrolatum, propylene glycol, quaternium-15, and vinyl chloride. All of these substances are petroleum derivatives, and they all add carbon to the environment, some of them in the form of greenhouse gases.

Check online to see where you can find sustainable products, including green home-cleaning kits with recipes for cleaning products made from common household items. Don't drink bottled water. Invest in a water filter and take your own bottled water on the road. Plastic bottles can take hundreds of years to degrade in the environment. Start to be part of the solution instead of the problem. After all, good planets are hard to find.

Glossary

biodiversity The variety and numbers of plant and animal species in the world or in a given habitat.

biosphere The world viewed as the sum total of all living organisms and their ecosystems.

brine Water containing large amounts of salt; ocean water, for example, is briny.

climatologist A scientist who studies climate and its related phenomena, including historical patterns of climate change.

conservationist A person who advocates and works for the conservation, or responsible management, of natural resources, including living species.

cryosphere Those areas or parts of the earth, most of which are found in the polar regions, that contain water in its frozen state: glaciers, ice sheets or caps, sea ice, permafrost, and the like.

fauna The animal life of a given geographical region.

flora The plant life of a given geographical region.

ecologist A scientist who studies ecosystems and their functioning.

ecosystem A group of living and nonliving things that interact dynamically in a given area.

endemic Referring to a species unique to a single location or region; that is, one found nowhere else on earth.

food web The feeding relationship between organisms in an ecosystem, starting with plant life and ending with animal life.

ice cap A thick ice layer, smaller than an ice sheet, built from compacted snow over the course of tens of thousands of years.

ice sheet An ice layer covering a land area larger than 20,000 square miles (50,000 km²).

indicator species Animal and plant species that reveal their status and provide information about the health of their ecosystem.

marine biologist A scientist who studies the various forms of ocean life and their interactions.

primatologist A scientist who studies primates.

salinization The buildup of salts—in topsoil, for example—from seawater infiltration or other causes.

thermal expansion The tendency of a material to expand when heated and contract when cooled. In seawater and other fluids, thermal expansion usually appears as an increase in volume.

vascular plants A higher-order plant with specialized tissues that allow the storage and transport of water and nutrients throughout the plant.

Notes

p. 5. ". . . changes are taking place in ecosystems . . .": Gian-Reto Walther et al., "Ecological responses to recent climate change," *Nature* 416 (2002): 389–395.

p. 10. ". . . the polar ice cap and the permanent ice cover shrinking at a rate of 9 percent per decade.": NASA Earth Science Gallery, http://www.nasa.gov/topics/earth/features/2012-seaicemin.html.

p. 10. M. C. Serreze, M. M. Holland, and J. Stroeve,"Perspectives on the Arctic's Shrinking Sea-Ice Cover," *Science* 315 (March 16, 2007): 1533–1536.

p. 10 "In Sept. 2012...in 2007." Arctic Sea Ice Hits Smallest Extent In Satellite Era, http://www.nasa.gov/topics/earth/features/2012-seaicemin.html.

p. 10. "NASA reports..." http://www.nasa.gov/topics/earth/features/2012-seaicemin.html.

p. 12. ". . . USGS study . . .": David H. Ward, Christian P. Dau, T. Lee Tibbitts, James S. Sedinger, Betty A. Anderson, James E. Hines, "Change in Abundance of Pacific Brant Wintering in Alaska: Evidence of a Climate Warming Effect?" *Arctic* 62, no. 3 (2009), http://www.usgs.gov/newsroom/article.asp?ID=2302.

p. 13. " In 1997 . . .": *Christian Science Monitor* article on a U.S. Geological Survey study, www.csmonitor.com/Environment/Global-Warming/2009/0923/warmer-alaska-winters-let-geese-skip-trip-south.

p. 14. "Recent data indicate . . .": L. S. Vors and M. S. Boyce, "Global Declines of Caribou and Reindeer," *Global Change Biology* 15, no. 11 (Nov. 2009): 2626–2633.

p. 15. ". . . the polar bear will be gone . . .": M. Owen and R. R. Swaisgood, "On Thin Ice: Climate Change and the Future of Polar Bears," *Biodiversity,* 9, nos. 3–4 (2008): 123–128.

p. 18. "The Antarctic continent is warming . . .": J. Turner et al., "Antarctic Climate Change During the Last 50 Years," *Int. J. Climatol.* 25 (2005): 279–294.

p. 18. "Air temperatures . . ." British Antarctic Survey, Antarctic Peninsula: Rapid Warming, www.antarctica.ac.uk/bas_research/science/climate/antarctic_peninsula.php.

p. 18. "With an average . . .": U.S. Antarctic Program, About the Continent, http://www.usap.gov/usapgov/aboutTheContinent/index.cfm?m=2.

p. 19. "Reports show that . . . to increased regional precipitation.": British Antarctic Survey, http://www.antarctica.ac.uk/bas_research/science/climate/climate_change.php.

p. 20. "Studies show . . . by 50 percent.": *National Geographic*, May 9, 2001, http://news.nationalgeographic.com/news/2001/05/0509_penguindecline.html.

p. 27. "The ocean waters . . . on our planet.": Seacology, http://www.seacology.org/about/importance.htm.

p. 28. "Marine biologists . . . ravages of the sea.": Seacology, http://www.seacology.org/about/importance.htm.

p. 36. "Glaciers contain almost . . . Earth." U.S. Geological Survey, http://ga.water.usgs.gov/edu/earthglacier.html.

p. 36. "The Himalayan glaciers . . .": Project Surya, http://www.projectsurya.org/water-food-security.

p. 38. "Many scientists predict . . .": Environmental Protection Agency, www.epa.gov/climatechange/science/futuretc.html.

p. 38. "Still-dry BC Burns Through 2010 Forest-Fire Budget," *Victoria Times Colonist*, August 5, 2010, p.A5.

p. 38. "Megafires are on the rise . . .": U.S. Forest Service news release August 17, 2011, http://www.fs.fed.us/news/2011/releases/08/wallow.shtml.

p. 39. "Researchers estimate . . . will go extinct.": C. H. Sekercioglu et al., "Climate Change, Elevational Range Shifts, and Bird Extinctions," *Conservation Biology* 22, no. 1 (Feb. 2008): 140-150.

p. 43. "A study in the Costa Rican protected area . . .": Whitfield, Bell, Phillippi, Sasa, Bolanos, Chaves, Savage, and Donnelly, "Amphibian and Reptile Declines Over 35 Years at

La Selva, Costa Rica," PNAS doi.0611256104, 2007.

p. 44. "From 1980 to 2000 . . . of tropical forests.": H. K. Gibbs et al., "Tropical Forests Were the Primary Sources of New Agricultural Land in the 1980s and 1990s," *PNAS* 107, no. 36 (Sept. 7, 2010).

p. 48. "...protected areas...2012." UNEP-WCMC. Cambridge, UK: Protected Planet Report 2012. www.wdpa.org.

p. 52. "Though natural . . . in the not-to-distant future." National Park Service Climate Change Response Program, Climate Change Overview, http://www.nature.nps.gov/climatechange.

Find Out More

Books

Anderson, Dale. *Al Gore: A Wake-up Call to Global Warming*. New York: Crabtree, 2009.

Franklin Watts Editors. *Is It Hot Enough for You: Global Warming Heats Up*. New York: Franklin Watts, 2009.

Hanel, Rachel. *Climate Fever: Stopping Global Warming*. Mankato, MN: Compass Point Books, 2010.

Nardo, Don. *Climate Crisis: The Science of Global Warming*. Mankato, MN: Compass Point Books, 2009.

Petersen, Christine. *Earth's Changing Climate*. New York: Marshall Cavendish Benchmark, 2011.

Spalding, Frank. *Catastrophic Climate Change and Global Warming*. NY: Rosen, 2010.

Weaver, Andrew. *Generation Us: The Challenge of Global Warming*. Raven Books, 2011.

Websites

Climate Change Education
This huge portal is for everyone, from teachers to students to families. It has hands-on science demonstrations, science equipment, and phone apps. There are also lesson plans and student projects. For one-stop shopping on everything about climate change and sustainable living, this is a good place to start.
http://climatechangeeducation.org/

Cool the Earth

This fun website provides climate change education for the whole family. Take an online tour of the program for K–8 students, and if you want to participate, support materials will be sent directly to your school.

www.cooltheearth.org/

EducaPoles—International Polar Foundation (IPF)

This educational website stresses the importance of the polar regions, particularly in relation to climate change. Teaching materials and activities, mainly targeting middle- and secondary-school students, include subjects ranging from sustainable development to biodiversity in the Arctic.

www.educapoles.org/

Seacology

The mission of this international, nonprofit organization is to save cultures, habitats, and endangered species on islands around the world. The site tracks the number of acres of island land it has protected as well as coral reefs and other marine habitats. Seacology is also actively building schools, community centers, and water-delivery systems for island inhabitants.

www.seacology.org/

Index

Page numbers in **bold** are photographs, illustrations, and maps.

About the Author

Stephen Aitken is fascinated by the natural world and its remarkable diversity. He is the author of many books for young people from third grade to high school, written for publishers all over the world. Aitken is a biologist and the senior editor of *Biodiversity*, a peer-reviewed science journal, and executive secretary of Biodiversity Conservancy International. He is a vegetarian, does not own a car, and tries to keep his carbon footprint as close to his shoe size as possible. Aitken's studio in the beautiful Himalayas of India provides shelter for ants and spiders, baby geckos, and an odd orange-eared mouse.

For a complete list of books Aitken has written and illustrated, please visit www.stephenaitken.com.